Angelspeake™

How to Talk with
Your Angels

A Guide

Barbara Mark
&
Trudy Griswold

Simon & Schuster

SIMON & SCHUSTER
Rockefeller Center
1230 Avenue of the Americas
New York, NY 10020

SIMON & SCHUSTER and colophon are registered trademarks
of Simon & Schuster Inc.

Designed by Levavi & Levavi

Manufactured in the United States of America

17 19 20 18 16

Library of Congress Cataloging-in-Publication Data
Mark, Barbara.
Angelspeake : how to talk with your angels : a guide /
Barbara Mark & Trudy Griswold.
p.   cm.
1. Angels.   2. Spiritual life.   I. Griswold, Trudy.   II. Title.
BL477.M36   1995
133.9'3—dc20   95-31311
CIP
ISBN 0-684-81547-8

Angelspeake® is a registered trademark of
Barbara Mark and Trudy Griswold.

Acknowledgments

We wish to thank each of these earthangels for their ceaseless encouragement. Each one of them helped in an important way as we learned to do the angels' work. Our path was easier because of their backing.

Patti Michels, who introduced us to the possibility of our work.

Winifred Clark, our spiritual mentor who helped us understand we were ready.

French Wallop for her generous two-week gift at the Canyon Ranch Lodge so we could have the perfect place to write *Angelspeake.*

Pat and Grigsby Markham, of the Windham Hill Inn, hosts of our first Angelspeake Seminar.

Roger and Bettybob Williams, who gave us our first computer.

Bill Kendall, aka "Saint Bill," our ever-patient computer genius.

Kathy Harrison for sharing her artistic gifts.

Opal Bohnsack, who helped us spread the angels' word.

Donna DeGutis, for her encouragement to continue with this book.

Lalia Madriguera, for her great ideas on how to share the angels' messages.

Judy Courtemanche, who always came through with what was needed at the right time.

Linda Engstrom, who kept saying we weren't crazy.

Molly Yowell, who at times thought we were crazy and supported us anyway.

Gillian Drummond, who taught us to remain true to our purpose and mission.

Judy Gilmour and her friend Jonathon with their trusted advice.

Donna Kremer, who never counts the cost of love.

Chris Heise, the best example we know of how the angels' love works on earth and in our lives.

Natalie Zilli, who fed our bodies while the angels fed our souls.

Frank Don, who gave us our first local exposure.

Roni Gregory, who first took us "on the road."

Rochelle Gordon, who first took our message nationally.

John Sammis and Ron Jaffe, who saw a much bigger picture than we had dreamed.

Andrew Ackemann, a significant link in the miracle of *Angelspeake* events.

Dominick Anfuso, the catalyst who made it possible for the angels' messages to spread worldwide.

Cassie Jones, who coordinated a million details to make sure *Angelspeake* became a reality.

And the many others who have helped in their special ways to show their love for us and the angels.

This book is dedicated to our families.

*To Dorothy and Frank Baber, who began this
remarkable family.
To Jackie Baber Anderson, our sister, who won't
let us take life too seriously.
To our children, Michael, Suzanne, and
Stephanie Mark, and Caroline and Katie Griswold,
who lovingly encouraged us as we walked our
spiritual path and who will carry the angels' work
into the future.
To Bob Griswold for his loyal support, his vision,
and his theological perspective.*

Contents

You are not led.
You are shown.
Then you desire
what you see.

Preparing for Angelspeaking

Angels are messengers from God. We have been taught that it is possible for people to easily receive the messages the angels carry from God. We are passing this information to you as we have to thousands of others in classes the angels have inspired us to teach.

Although this book is not a substitute for your personal religious beliefs, it is meant to enhance every part of your life and we lovingly pass on the angels' teachings to you as they have taught us. Belief in and contact with angels is consistent with all traditional religions. Our words will be written in regular type style. Italicized paragraphs will indicate thoughts and teachings dictated by angels.

Expect miracles to happen from this moment forward. For angels work in miracles.

It all starts from God. Pray for His love to surround you, and enjoy meeting your angels.

*It is our mission to teach
you to hear us.
Our mission is to help you
find your mission.*

Introduction

Until August of 1991, our lives were going along like everyone else's. Then the angels woke us up. Everything changed . . . forever.

We are sisters who were raised in Iowa in a traditional small town. There were three daughters, plus a mom and a dad. We went to Sunday school as kids and after we were married and had our own children, we taught Sunday school. We believed in God and prayed when it seemed right. We were uncommonly close as sisters and considered ourselves to be basically normal American women, concerned with family, home, and career.

Trudy lived and raised her kids in Connecticut, Barbara in Wyoming. Later, after her children were grown, Barbara divorced and moved to San Diego. Trudy still lives in Connecticut. Good times and bad times came and went and lessons were learned. We lived on a daily basis as most people do.

But in both of us, a sense of longing was growing. A sense of knowing there was something we *needed* to do with our lives that was very important for us to do and it was coming closer.

We became seekers. We began to attend lectures and seminars and read many self-help and spiritual books. The unsettled feeling grew.

The first contact came one morning as Barbara was sleeping.

"The angels woke me up, literally. From a sound sleep, I was awakened and the angels said," *Get a pencil and paper and we'll write to you.*

"I said, 'No!' I didn't want to wake up at that hour and didn't want to leave my comfortable bed. Finally, I reluctantly found some paper, returned to bed, and wrote what was dictated to me. Here is the first message I received."

Peace begins inside. Until you find peace there, there is no peace. Money will come. Keep the faith. It is just another lesson. No different from the others. The right people are here to help you—on both sides. Be gentle with yourself. Be in the now. You did well yesterday. Enjoy today. Go to church. Eat well. Walk. Do what you love. We are sending you love.

"I did not think it was a particularly important message, but I loved the feeling that surrounded the delivery of it. I felt safe and loved and went back to sleep. This was the first of almost daily messages I received. Most of them teaching or comforting me.

"But no matter how comforting, how loving, and how accurate the messages, I couldn't believe that divine angels were communicating with me. 'It must be my imagination,' I thought. Or, 'My God, am I going crazy?' I can't tell you how many times I called my sister (she's the analytical one) with doubts, questions, fears about what was happening and where these messages were coming from."

Then, several months later, Trudy was awakened.

"My heart was beating out of my chest when I felt the angels' energy coming through me. I knew immediately what it was, but didn't know how to access it. So, I picked up a pen and paper, sat up in my bed, and began writing.

" 'Dearest Angels, my sister Barbara says that it is now time for me to write to you on my own' " . . . *and we are so glad you have decided to come to us today, for this is the day our connection is to be made. It is now time for us to start our work together. Thank you for your trust and your willingness to communicate with us. More will be given. Write to us often and know we love you and are always here to comfort you.*

Now we both were receiving messages. We asked who they were.

Our energy comes directly from God. It is a sound energy. A vibratory energy that spirit can attune itself to. You cannot hear it on your plane. It is part of the electronic bands in the spectrum (whatever that meant).

We don't know when they began to call themselves "angels." It wasn't a surprise when they did. We knew this is what they were, and as they explained who they were to us, we accepted them as angels. We received messages concerning past activities and our future life's work. Page after page of information was given to us. Every time we sat down, we found we could access them and their wisdom. To us it seemed like a miracle.

From our first communications, our lives began to change. One of the first important things we learned was to *trust* the messages. We asked hundreds of questions. We doubted. We tested. We spent hours on the telephone trying to figure out what was coming to us, from whom, and why to us. We could not stop the messages from coming. We were being taught daily about God, the universe, love, and about our paths.

Before long we both began to receive messages

to teach others how to speak with their angels. "But who will come?" we asked. "People will think we're crazy." But the message kept coming with increasing force and frequency. Finally, friends began to ask us to explain what we were doing, and if *they* had angels and if *they* could learn how to talk with their own angels. We decided that it was okay to share what we had learned with our close friends, who were, after all, asking us lots of questions about the angels. At worst, our good friends wouldn't think we were totally crazy—so we began.

We asked what we were to teach, and received an entire lesson plan. The angels assured us they would bring students to us, and Barbara's first class in California had seventeen people. Trudy's in Connecticut had thirty-five! We taught what the angels had taught us and continue to do just that today. Even the name of our classes and of this book—*Angelspeake*—came from them.

You may ask, "Why would anyone want to talk to their angels?" In learning this process of connecting with your angels you will also learn of the many dimensions of love and support that are available to you. You are a spiritual being currently having a physical experience on earth. This book has been written to teach you to communicate with your angels through writing, in order to reconnect your spiritual and physical selves.

Communicating with the angels through writing *feels* wonderful, too. You not only feel truth when you are told a message, you also feel unconditional love when you receive it yourself. It is the difference between a candle and sunlight, the difference between a seed and a tree. It is the difference between doubt and joy! It is the major reason for this book.

This book was also written to teach you how to contact your angels and to satisfy your curiosity if you have been awakened *already* and don't know what happened or why. Many students come to us, not to learn to write, but to understand from where the messages they have received have come.

After being on *Good Morning America* we knew a book had to be written for you who also seek from far away. The format of *Angelspeake* follows the classes we teach. This book is primarily for you who are not near a class. We have written this book as simply as possible, without frills or fluff. By the time you put this book down, we want you to be able to *connect* with your angels. It is so easy!

Barbara and Trudy

Angels will

Care for you,

Love you,

Teach you.

You are worth it!

Many of you are being awakened today to hear our messages and to believe in our help and support, our *practical* help and support. As you go throughout your day, we are there. We are not hiding, or difficult to feel or to know. We are always with you and we are *always* available. Now.

*What holds humans in
limitation is their
Preference for the Past,
Desire for the Future,
and Avoidance of
the Now.*

chapter 1

Who Are Angels?

God is . . .

It all starts with God. Keep the God you have. You do not have to change the God you know to understand the angels. God is God. Don't mistake Him for another being. All we know to tell you about God is what the angels have told us.

No matter how big, huge, all-consuming, or wise you think God is . . . you do not have Him big enough. Not nearly big enough. God is Love, The Father, The Mother, The Source, The All, Allah, The Divine Mind, The Supreme Being, The Goddess. Whatever you have learned to call Him or Her, God is the one we <u>all</u> pray to. Even we angels.

In our classes, students want to know what kinds of angels come to them when they write. For the most part, angels fall into several main categories. A long time ago an ancient scholar named Dionysius was given the Three Hierarchies and the Nine Choirs of Angels. Each of these groupings of angels has a commitment to God and works within His kingdom, carrying out His plan and will.

The angels in the hierarchy closest to the earth are dedicated to working with us while we are here.

We will focus on the groups of angels who will be teaching you the most frequently: angels, guardian angels and archangels, who are all divine beings.

Angels were created by God to be His messengers, to do His will, and to help humankind. Angels are divine beings from God who watch over you and guide you and keep you safe. This group includes many levels of angels assigned to provide help, support, and comfort. Angels have never lived on earth. They are not and never have been human. As a cow is different from a person, so an angel is different. Angels are unique beings and, after God, have the greatest view of the total purpose of earth, its inhabitants, and the universe.

Archangels are God's emissaries to give to earth love and compassion. As you are thinking about your spiritual path, you might want to call on the influence of one or more archangels. They will help you increase your learning and strength.

Many people believe there are seven archangels. There are more, but those named below have been assigned to earth to help us while we are on our planet.

Michael: From the Hebrew, his name means "Who is like God." Michael battles evil, challenges people who have evil or negative intentions, and helps people open up to new ways of thinking, bringing courage for spiritual experiences.

Raphael: This archangel's name means "God has overcome." He works with healers and artists and is helpful to creative souls. Messages from Raphael may help you to focus on creating a space of beauty, a recognition of the beauty that surrounds you, and the healing energy that comes from embracing such beauty.

Gabriel: Most often associated with a trumpet, his name means "Man of God." Gabriel announces God's plans and actions. He brought forth the news of Jesus. He will tell you about your path and purpose and will send help to complete your mission.

Uriel: "Fire of God." Archangel of Prophecy. Uriel helps you complete your goals and your life missions. If you get off-center while on your spiritual path, you can expect new thoughts and transforming ideas from Uriel.

Haniel: "Mercy of God." The nicest things of life are watched over by Haniel. Beauty, love, happiness, pleasure, and harmony are his domain.

Raziel: "Secret of God." Archangel of Mysteries. Questions and mysteries encountered while on our spiritual journey inspire us to dig deeper in search of divine knowledge. As we seek, Raziel may come through with inspirations and ideas that unlock the truths we are seeking.

Auriel: "Light of God." The angel most closely associated with our future and our purpose and goals.

Guardian Angels were assigned to you personally and are always with you. Other angels may come and go as needed, but your guardian is one hundred percent committed to you for your entire life.

Angels will not run your life. No angel will intrude on your free will. They cannot interfere. The key to receiving help from any angel is to ask for it. They will always be evident when you ask for their assistance. Even though you may be in imminent danger, they pray to God for you and will only go to work if it is God's will to do so.

We never work singly! If you see just one of us, know there are thousands of backup helpers. We always come as a Heavenly Choir of Love. What you need to perceive for your greatest good is what you will perceive.

Every essence, thought, or feeling has a corresponding angel. Whatever your need, there are angels ready to bring help. When you are in a dentist's chair, ask for the Angel of Fearlessness to be with you. Perhaps an Angel of Strength and an Angel of Patience, or an Angel of Calmness. For the dentist, ask for Angels of Steadiness, Swiftness, Painlessness, and Wisdom to guide his hands. Ask for anything you want to have happen, and an angel will be there *immediately* to blend with your personal energy.

Most of us have been conditioned to think angels look like seventeenth-century paintings. In reality, angels have all sorts of appearances. This excerpt from our soon to be published children's book, *God Invented Angels First,* explains best what angels look like.

God invented angels before He made
everything else.
Angels are God's helpers and messengers.
They tell people what God wants them to
know.
There are all kinds of angels.
Big angels. Little angels.
Boy angels. Girl angels.
And some angels you don't know what they are.
Some angels have wings. Some don't have wings.

Some wings are VERY BIG. *Some are teeny tiny.*
All angels have halo light around them.
This is their energy showing and it is very beautiful.
Angels have names.
Some have important-sounding fancy names.
Some have names like yours.
Ask your angel what its name is. Your angel
will tell you.
Yes, you can talk to your angel. It is very easy to
chat with an angel.
Angels are always with you to listen and visit
with you.
Angels even will talk back to you.

The truth of angels is they have many shapes, forms, sizes, appearances, and duties. No one angel is like another. You will see angels as you need to see them. Sometimes you may see only a burst of light in a darkened room or a cloudy form around a person's body. Often angels will appear as a recognizable human, perhaps even someone you know or have known of. Other times they will transform into a symbol that you will understand. Need a warrior? Ask for one. Need some joy in your life? An angel can bring it to you.

Sometimes you will connect with beings who are not angels in the classic sense but souls who have lived on earth and who now can teach from the other side. Many people also refer to this group as angels, although in the strictest sense of the word they are not truly angels, even though they also work for God.

Masters and spirit guides are wise, elevated souls who have usually lived on earth as human beings. Often they are recognizable, such as Jesus, a saint, or a biblical character. If you belong to a religion or group with a loving head or teacher, this master may appear to you.

Masters and spirit guides are the majority of beings who will be coming to you with messages. They frequently teach and are here to help you with your life problems and lessons to keep you on your path. Because they have lived on earth they have compassion and understand your problems. They are committed to your life and understand you even more than you do. They know how you are interconnected with other souls. They know your life goals and can see into your future. They protect you, warn you, and love you.

This also includes the groups known as teachers, guides, and ascended masters. They have different personalities and appearances and constantly remind you of your strengths, virtues, purpose, and lovingness. Masters and spirit guides are workers and teachers.

Many Catholics feel especially close to a saint.

Jews may relate well with a prophet, while Hindus revere one or more gurus. Whatever your religious background or belief, expect many personalities and interesting contacts when you are working with masters.

Barbara's main guide is the Old Testament Joshua. While on the earth, Joshua was a warrior, and he comes to Barbara as a no-nonsense guide and fierce protector.

Trudy's guardians go by the name John-Paul. These are two energies who have joined together to be her master teachers. John was a healer and disciple of Jesus. Paul was a teacher. Trudy's work this lifetime is to be a healer-teacher, and these energies help her with this work.

Because you are spiritual beings having a physical experience this lifetime, when your earthwork is done you will pass over to the other side, join the angels, and help those still on earth.

Deceased mortals are those who have made their transition from the earthplane to afterlife. These are simply people who have died. They are not ghosts, though they are sometimes mistaken for them. They are souls with whom you can communicate in the same way you did when on the earth together. They may be a spouse, parent, grandparent, or friend, and they are frequently recognizable.

Our biological father comes to us occasionally when we need loving support. We can tell it's him because he smells like Dad, and we physically experience his essence and presence.

We are a heavenly choir of Love.

We recognize our mother because she kisses our cheeks when she is with us. The sense of unconditional love we feel has brought us to tears as we experience the true and total love of Mom.

Some of us have relatives and friends we do not care to see again—on any side of life. But we assure you, that beings who have died or "gone to the light" *are* now beings of light and will not bring you anything but love. When the body dies, the part of the person that was cranky, or mean, or unloving does not make the transition to the light. Painful and negative earth energy stays behind on the earth. Therefore, when you meet up with a "dead relative"—even if they were despicable on earth—you will meet them only as the love they have become. They become a form of pure and unconditional love that will be a transforming experience for you when you encounter it.

Less than loving entities that show up are NOT of the angels. Such entities are not welcome, and you should invite them out firmly, just as you would an unwanted guest in your home. Prayer is the best method of allowing only loving, positive energy to come to you. Always pray before seeking spiritual contact.

Angels have the most universal knowledge and the most broad perspective. Masters are superb teachers with access to your innermost thoughts as they relate to the world. A deceased mortal's best work is done through unconditional love and comfort.

We call all the groups "angels." With a collective, small "a." There is an infinite number of angels, masters, spirit guides, and teachers. Most often you will not have any idea as to the type of "angel" you are receiving. This is fine. It is not so important WHO you receive, but only that you ARE receiving and that it touches your truth. You will learn from all of them.

Your **higher self** is your most perfect and knowledgeable you. Your higher self is not the angels, even though your higher self frequently comes to you as guidance. It is a combination of wisdom of all that you are, all that you have been and ever will be.

You are body, mind, and spirit. All three parts of you grow in different stages. A healthy higher self looks like an equilateral triangle. If one side grows too fast, the other sides have to catch up. Your higher self takes care of the balance.

It is us. The angels. We have become your teachers. There is a whole group of us on this side who are here for you. We are not here to run your life. We are not here to tell you what to do. Our purpose is to give you perspective. This perspective is not only from our level, but from the perspective of the larger picture, the greater meaning, which will give you a new form of guidance. We are called angels because the real meaning of our work is to be messengers of God. We are here to help carry out His plan, to be a support to those who seek, and to always give unconditional love. Your highest good is always first and foremost with us.

*Ask us for something for
yourself every day.
We long to give you gifts
from the universe.*

chapter 2

The
Four
Fundamentals

How to Begin

Frank, a Realtor friend of Barbara's, called and asked if she was still talking to "those dead people." When Barbara said yes, she still talked to the angels, her friend said, "Great, because I need a business plan by Monday." Barbara wasn't sure the angels did "business plans," but told Frank to come over anyway.

Frank told an awful tale of business woe. He needed to meet with some important businessmen on Monday to avoid foreclosure on a client's property. He knew it would be a struggle and believed the outcome would not be satisfactory.

During the reading, a wise angel gave Frank his business plan. This master also gave Frank, and the rest of you, Four Fundamentals for Living Successfully: Ask, Believe, Keep Your Mouth Shut, and Say Thank You.

Frank went to his business meeting on Monday with the Four Fundamentals in mind. The outcome of the negotiation was much better than he had expected, but his partner and wife was the most amazed one. She said, "I couldn't believe it when you were so quiet!" The Four Fundamentals had worked!

There is a fundamental formula for attracting the things you want and desire into your life. This simple formula is a means of approaching life each day in order to allow the right people, places, or things to come into your life. When your life is working well and the right things are coming to you, it is more than happiness. It is a state of being. A state of success!

People want proof that we are there. That we have validity. This formula for successful living is the easiest way to test us. To learn to trust us whether you want a parking place or a BMW to put in it, an A in algebra, or peace of mind, we can help. With this simple method, you can literally enhance any facet of your life. The way to success is to Ask for what you want, Believe it will be given, Let the process work, and to say Thank you.

Ask

Be specific. Asking does several things. First, it helps you focus on what you want. Clarity is the key to formulating what you would like to have. It is a decision to receive. Asking connects you with God and helps you see that all which is right for you comes from Him and that He is truly the one to whom you are directing your requests. We are taught from babyhood to "be careful what you ask for, you just might get it." But babies ask clearly, persistently, and loudly when they need something. You do the same. ASK BIG! Be positive. Ask for a lot! Don't ask for less than you want. Do not ask for a tent if you want a house. Don't ask for a C if you want an A. Above all, don't ask for half a gift. Be specific, and then more specific. Angels are empowered to bring you help in every area of your life. Even the material.

Think of something you want. A car is a good example to think about because nearly everyone wants a car that is different or better than the one they have. If you just say, "I want a car" or "I WANT A CAR," your angels do not have enough information. Imagine a loving and giving being with all that the world has to offer standing behind you. Every car in the world is available for this being to bring you. This being or angel needs to know *what* car you have decided to have.

Pretend you are ordering from a catalogue and all sorts of information is being requested on the order form. Fill in the blanks for size, color, material, amount. Exactly what kind of car do you decide to give yourself? Write down every option that is important to you and then decide to have it! BE SPECIFIC AND ASK BIG!

Free will enters in here. Angels won't intrude. If you do not ask, angels cannot and will not act except in times of peril. Asking opens the door. Only after you make the invitation can they help. The asking may be very quick, but it is there. If this sounds punitive, remember that God has given humankind the gift of free will. This is how to use it to have the angels help you.

Believe

After you have asked for what you would like to come into your life, your next step is to **believe** and trust that if it is the right thing for you, if it is part of your plan for being here, then it will happen. This can be very difficult for some. Trust and belief are the underlying elements of letting things happen in the correct way and knowing that God and you together have a plan in mind. Allow the angels to work for your greatest good and believe they will bring it to you.

Some things you ask for do not affect your life-work, such as asking for parking places or ease of finding items when you are shopping. Angels give this help freely and are genuinely pleased to help make your life easier. Angels also give little gifts like keeping the green light green and helping you remember your mother's birthday. All these are ways angels work in your life.

So, ask for that scholarship. Ask for your perfect mate to appear. Ask for parking places and pickup trucks and eighteen-speed mountain bikes. Ask for your lost ring to be found. Ask for a free vacation in the mountains. Ask for what you have decided to have and then expect and believe it shall be given if it is for your greater good. The angels do not try to hold anything from you.

Let It Happen

Originally the angels told Frank to *Keep your mouth shut.* For the rest of us, they translate this step to read, **Let It Happen.** This step requires patience, and human patience is not very deep.

There will be a temptation to meddle. Letting it happen is the hardest part. Letting go is allowing the angels to work. It is also proof that you *believe*. You do not need to repeat, worry, over-think, or beg. It is like letting bread rise—the more you disturb it, the less it will happen. Let it be. Just expect positive results and ask the angels to help you.

Thank You

Once you have asked for something, believed and trusted you will receive it for your greater good, and then let go of the process and outcome, it is time to **give thanks** to God for His will being done. Giving thanks closes the loop on your request and reinforces the third step, letting it happen. It frees you to move on with what's important and keeps you active in your path rather than passive while you await a specific event.

This method is a means of empowering yourself. Materialism is different and comes from negative attitudes. These four positive fundamental steps for spiritual living teach you it's okay to ask. It's okay to believe. It's okay to have. The higher your self-worth and self-esteem, the easier you will find this to be true. If you cannot ask the angels for what you need and desire, then how can you ask your boss for a raise? You are worthy of all that is.

Speaking with us is easier than you can believe if you use the principles in this success formula.

Ask us to be with you.
Believe that we are with you and that you will receive a message.
Let it happen and begin writing what you know to write.
After your message is received, acknowledge it with a Thank you.

When you begin to use these fundamental rules, you will notice immediate changes in your life. Not just in having more material abundance either. We will seem more companionable, active, and real. Our energy will feel good to you. Fear and loneliness will disappear. You will begin to talk to your angels. Out loud. You will become trusted friends. People will begin to see your changes in beauty, happiness, and peace. Life will work better, and peace will shine from your face. Joy and Success will be yours!

Because you learned to read, you can now read all the books. Because you learn to hear us, you can now hear all the angels.

chapter 3

The Seven Steps to Talk with Your Angels

The Four Fundamentals worked! We told everyone how easy it was to ask the angels for help. Our own experiences were proving to us that the angels were practical assistants, and our families began calling us and asking us for help with their requests. We felt quite important for a while, but then it began to seem as though everyone we were related to had to call us before making any kind of a decision. It became commonplace to pick up the phone and have someone ask us to ask the angels

41

for help with some "necessity" or for a writing from the angels to help with a problem.

Then, wisely, the angels gave us a list of people we could no longer do writings for. They told us that these individuals' own abilities were developed and they could talk to the angels for themselves.

This was not a popular proclamation. To a person, the cry was, "I don't know how! This is your gift, not mine!" When we asked for guidance, the angels said that everyone had the ability to talk with their angels directly. If this was true, then we wanted, and needed, instructions to teach people how to access them.

The Four Fundamentals for spiritual living were, by now, a part of our lives. So we asked the angels for help. We believed and trusted we would receive instruction, and when we let it happen, these simple step-by-step guidelines came through in a teaching. Seekers could now follow a simple method to connect with their angels themselves.

We wrote, "Angels, how does one learn this skill?"

Practice, practice, practice. Just as you have learned anything. Pray for guidance, insight. Remain open to the skill and allow it to come to you. Remember, all knowledge is already within you. All you need to do is access it. When you are learning, you are doing nothing more than remembering what you already know. Skill comes with repetition as in flying an airplane. You can already know how to fly an airplane in your brain. The skill comes through the practice of it. Knowledge will come to you in many ways. Through study. Through dreams. Through experience. All will be there for you when you manifest the desire. In order to connect with us in writing, all you need do is pray, breathe, listen, write, accept, follow your inner knowing, and trust.

Pray . . .

for the truth

and the

gift of

spiritual

hearing

Step 1: Pray

Ask to be a clear channel and keep yourself out of it. Pray for the truth and the gift of spiritual hearing.

Praying will also put you in the white light of divine grace and love. This is both a protection and a connection with your angels.

Prayer is an invitation to God to come to you. It is a simple method of asking. Many lessons have been given on the power of prayer. It is the power of *asking* that is the true message. The means and method of prayer open the links between man and God. The angels become part of your energy with this invitation.

It does not matter what you pray. It is the intention that starts the energy flow. Many adults still start their praying with their childhood prayers of comfort: "Now I lay me down to sleep . . ." can be just as comforting to an eighty-year-old as it is to a child.

Use the invitation you like best. Some people's prayers are short. Others enjoy the rhythm of many words repeated over and over in sequence. Imagine a big lens on your chest. As you pray, feel it open wider and wider, letting in more light and freshness. This is a preparation for God to enter after the invitation is given.

Prayer is an attitude. A charming attitude of peace, joyous reception, and love. Even in times of upheaval or periods of pain and doubt, prayer still has this same attitude. Prayer opens the doors of your heart.

Breathe . . .

be of

serene

nature

Step 2: Breathe

Sit and relax. Breathe and become open. Do not meditate. But also do not activate. Just be of serene nature.

Keep your eyes open. Meditation is a deeper physical state that is too relaxed for this purpose. Strive for a state of relaxed attention similar to the same energy you use while driving a car or watching television.

The angels come into you through air. They are spirit, and in order to enter into your body, they first surround your being with energy. They slide into your cells through your breath.

People tend to be shallow breathers. Concentrate on longer and slower breaths rather than short little breaths. If you want to know what the energy of breathing deeply feels like, put a straw in your mouth and inhale slowly. Then exhale. Breathe in through your straw again. The purpose is not to hyperventilate, but to know what it feels like to open your lungs to the bottom. Think of divine energy coming in on the inhale and think of each exhale as making room for more love to enter you.

When your breathing is correctly balanced, you will feel each breath as being cool energy like water flowing through a glass tube. It is the best and most pure freshness. Enjoy the breathing you do. As much as you enjoy quenching your thirst with water, quench your spiritual longing with air.

Breathe now. The angels are with you. This is their *love* you feel.

Listen . . .

we come to

you

as a whisper

Step 3: Listen

We come to you as a whisper. Soft and gentle. It will seem as your own thoughts, but we will stop and start. If you hear three words, type or write the three words. There may be a pause before the next words, but they will come. Do not force it, us, or you.

The angels ARE communicating with you in one way or another. It is the very same "voice" that has been guiding you all your life. The "voice" that reminds you to turn off the iron. The "voice" that says to change lanes on the highway.

Sometimes the message comes to you as a feeling or "knowing." A translation process occurs. It is like Morse code. Energy is sent and you intuitively know how to interpret its meaning. Occasionally, when you begin to become more aware, you may seem to hear more clearly, see colors more intensely, or feel a strong sense of energy around you or flowing through you. Sometimes people feel afraid of this intensity, but a sensory experience can be a natural part of the process.

Listening is also an attitude of openness. Think of communication as a radio. You cannot see one sound wave. But you know they are there. A receptive attitude is the "on" switch. You are not going to hear anything different than you already have. You are just going to realize that, when you pay attention by listening or receiving, the communications make sense.

Relax into the experience, but not too deeply. Just as when you listen to a symphony, you enjoy the music more by listening actively. And this is a beautiful symphonic experience.

Write . . .

the

harder

you think the

less flow

there

will be

Step 4: Write

*Hear the words come just a second before they are
written. You will hear. Do not worry about it making*

sense. You do not have to go into some spiritual state. Just write what you hear as you hear it. Sometimes you will receive "thought sentences" where you know what you are going to write in total, like a story you know already or a phrase you frequently use. The harder you think, the less flow there will be.

The angels call this process of taking information **automatic dictation.** Automatic dictation is simply recording the information as it is being given to you through your thoughts. You write what you hear or know to write. You are fully conscious, aware, and in control of yourself. Don't confuse this with automatic writing, which is a different method entirely. In dictation, you are fully conscious of what is being given to you. In automatic writing, you are not aware of the information as it is being sent.

Trudy received her first message by just beginning to write her own thoughts. The angels interrupted her with their message. Asking a short question helps others.

Hand-writing messages is the most common method, but if you have a typewriter or computer, you will find the messages can be received more quickly and easily. There is no incorrect way to receive a message. The key is to *begin.* Your favorite style of receiving will come later.

Accept...

the most

important

part

Step 5: Accept

What you write is what you write. We are guiding you but it will feel as though you are making it up. <u>It</u>

may always feel as though you are making it up. Acceptance is the most important part.

Of course you think you are making it up! They are sending you messages that filter through your life experiences, your brain, your personality, your vocabulary, and your memories. No one less than a divine being could communicate with you in this manner because no one on earth knows you this well. Angels remember situations and stories you have long ago forgotten. They know your pains, your strengths, and your inner truth. They feel your essence as much as their own. Angels are your most loyal friends and honest supporters. You do not even know this much about yourself.

Yes, you feel as though you are making it up because God in heaven is speaking to you, through the angels, to the God within you. All within a second.

You know it isn't you when you receive poetry, or song lyrics, or messages from a deceased relative. Messages like this could never be made up by you and you realize it is beyond your own experience.

At times you may doubt or question, but remember: the messages are never unloving, unkind, or mean. They are pure angel love.

Inner

Knowing...

it just comes

Step 6: Inner Knowing

There will be an absence of ego involved. You will not have to "think" about it or "plan" it as you would a paper. It just comes. You will find you don't remember what you wrote after you wrote it. It will always seem fresh.

Read the angel information in italics again. We cannot make this point more clear or use words any better. **You don't have to "think" about it. You don't have to "plan" it. It just comes.**

Even though your brain is insisting it is you, your heart knows differently. Angels are totally without ego. They are honest, sometimes silly, or are poor spellers, and some even have accents. You never talk to yourself as they do. They are much nicer.

By all means, keep all your angel messages and from time to time go back to your writings and reread them. If you already keep a journal or diary, you may want to buy a separate journal just for angel messages. However, you might find you have already been receiving angel writings and not even known it.

It is hard to explain how every part of this communication works. Just know that energy is transferred in an exchange of love and trust and that it will happen again and again if desired.

This is not a fluke. Receiving messages is like most things in life—the longer you do it, the better and more clear the messages become.

Inner Knowing is a combination of inner peace about the truth of the content of the messages you receive, and the realization that the angels' communication with you is loving, supporting, and only for your greater good. There becomes a longing to know more.

Trust . . .

these are

spiritual

gifts

Step 7: Trust

What we tell you is the best information we have at the time you receive it. We do not want to run your life.

This is a guidance to speed you along and to teach you skills you will need in your life's work. These are spiritual gifts. You did not have to do anything to get them. More will be given as you progress. Do not dissect for accuracy. Free will and different time tables create different patterns similar to ocean currents.

You are being asked by your angels for a little bit of time to trust the process of speaking to them. To just do it! It is the best gift God can give you.

Angels are constant. Angels don't experience life, death, or time as you do. Angels work in synchronicity, not in time frames. You *are* their work. Their existence is entirely to support, guide, love, and protect you. The more you visit with them and listen to them, the more helpful they will be and the easier it will be to access them. They are different from your chattering mind. They are more focused. Trust that what you hear is from them!

Above all, dear ones, know that this is the most loving thing we can do for you and we want you to succeed even more than you do. We will help you grow as fast as it is necessary for you to grow this lifetime. We will do all within our power to aid you through loving education and support.

*Say to yourself
each day . . .
At this moment
I trust the eternal
wisdom of the universe.
God is guiding my
every step and is
surrounding me with
love and protection.
I am doing His will.*

chapter 4

Making It Work

———— ✦ ————

Using the Four Fundamentals is most helpful when you are getting started. Ask us to be with you. Believe and trust you will receive a message. Let it happen and begin writing what you know to write. We will even say Thank you when we connect, for we truly want this connection more than you do, dear children.

Think of the acronym KISS. To us it means:
Keep It Simple, Seeker.

This whole process is simple and easy. We caution you against complicating it. Many people come to this process thinking there must be something magical involved or that it is going to be really hard, or that only "certain" people can communicate with their angels. We assure you, it is not any of the above!

In Chapter 3 we mentioned journaling and that some people buy a journal they use only for angel messages. There are several advantages in using a journal. All your angel messages are kept together chronologically. You will be able to go back and reread every message you have received. You will see your progress in continuity of thought and there might be a sequential pattern to the information. Your messages will seem new to you every time you read them.

Don't ritualize this process. You don't *need* any paraphernalia such as crystals, beads, candles, or music to receive what is coming through. All you need is a willingness to let the angels "in," no matter where you are. You can be in the middle of a store, driving down the road, or in the shower. Just allow the energy through. The angels will be there.

How to Begin:

Find a comfortable place in which to sit and relax. It might be on the floor, in a comfortable or favorite chair, or at the kitchen table. Many write sitting up in bed. It does not matter where you are as long as you can center yourself, take several deep breaths, and say a short prayer.

Prayer is ASKING. The Guardian Angel Prayer is used by children all over the world.

Guardian Angel Prayer

Angel of God, my guardian dear,
To whom God's love commits me here.
Ever this day be at my side,
To light and guard, to rule and guide.

Another prayer example is:

Dear God,
Please help me to hear you clearly
through your loving angels. Allow me to be
healed in my areas of greatest need and to learn
more about your truth, love, and joy.

Question:

Asking a question of the angels is also helpful as you begin writing. The question helps you focus, and the question will start the energy.

Some suggested questions that helped us:

Dear Angels, What would you like
to teach me today?

or

Dear Angels, Please tell me about my strengths.

Now you have begun! *Breathe,* open yourself to

be in an active, receptive place. Begin writing *any-thing* and *everything* that comes to your mind. Some people hear single words. Others see images or pictures, or receive thought sentences. Still others have a sense of just knowing. It doesn't matter what you receive, begin writing. Remember this is automatic dictation. It is not coming from you, so don't think about it or attempt to reorganize it.

No matter what happens, write! Sometimes the act of writing anything at all will allow the angels to "interrupt." What started out as your writing ends up as their message. You cannot make a mistake. There is no right or wrong way to do it. Angels do not scare off, so don't worry that they may run away.

If you have questions about the meaning of the message given to you . . . ask. This is a two-way communication, so feel free to get a dialogue going.

Angels' Names:

While you are writing, ask for the name of the angel who is talking. You will be amazed at the names you will hear. Even though angels don't necessarily have gender, you may feel as though male or female energy is there and you refer to the angel as "he" or "she." You may hear a name generally assumed to be male or female or you may also receive a group name.

Barbara's main group is Shining River et al. They named themselves that way because they are clean and pure and flow through her like water. Michael and the Many come to Trudy's husband. Trudy receives from Paul and the All. Other angel names we have heard include: Your Heavenly Hosts. The Angelic Chorus. Beings from the Universe. The Complete Ones. The angels have many identities and the names they give are part of the joy of communicating with them.

As you grow more confident in the messages, you will find there is little need to identify the angel who is speaking. You will simply trust the message as being true, loving, and pure no matter from whom it comes. This may be why angels often use group names for a signature.

Computer Writing:

Some people enjoy using their word processor or computer to receive messages. When we started to write to our angels more frequently, the information came so rapidly that we couldn't take down the message in longhand. The angels actually suggested we move to the computer to receive our messages as fast as possible. Even if you do not know how to type that well, you will be amazed at how quickly you'll be able to take down what the angels have to say. There is a lot of information for them to teach!

When Barbara first began using her computer, Trudy commented, "I didn't know you could type that fast." Barbara responded, "I can't."

Finally, remember you are not the first person to connect with an angel. People have been doing it for centuries!

Your earth is truly going through a spiritual evolution or revolution. Know this.
You personally are seeking and alive.
You are connected to your path.
We love you and are here to help you.
All you have to do is ask!

Typical Angel Messages:

First messages are often very simple. Reaching from one dimension to another is similar to adjusting a television set. It takes a little work, but once you are "tuned in" you will enjoy the reception immensely. Here are sample first messages.

TO ROSIE:
Dear One. The message will come. Relax. Don't force. Rest is important. The time has come. You will hear.

TO KEN:

Dear Child, don't be so impatient. Slow your mind to listen to us. You are here to listen, not to speak.

TO JANICE:

Yes, dear one, we are here. We want you to know we are always with you. We love you. Do not be afraid. We accept you.

TO LILA:

I love you. I am here. Do not be afraid. I will guide you. Loosen up. Learn.

Holy One. Yes, I am here.

Sometimes first readings are merely a series of words. With practice, these words fill out and become sentences.

TO MAUREEN (who had just stopped smoking):

Care
Clean
Air

The shortest message ever received in a class was this:

?????

The receiver assured us she knew exactly what it meant!

Sometimes you will receive a longer message the first time you write.

TO PATRICIA:

We love you and no matter what you do, we will continue to love you. Listen, listen, listen. Be still and listen. Do not be so hard on yourself. Love yourself as you love others. More later!

TO STEPHANIE:

Love Frank. Love Rebecca and Alex. Love yourself. Safe trip. Good business. Cheerfulness. Healing is here!

TO JOAN:

You are here today to experience and to grow in acceptance and love. You need to move forward on the journey. Jump-start each other and ask for help. It's easy! Today is a new start. Things will change for each of you. Do not expect to leave here the same person you were when you entered. You are different.

TO ARLENE:

My dear child, you are here tonight to share with others, to listen, to grow, to learn. You are on the right path. Just keep an open mind. Ask and you shall receive. This is just the beginning. The word will be spreading far and near. You are loved. Keep the faith.

TO BEN:

We are joyful that you are on your spiritual path and are focusing on the work. This work will trans-

form your life and bring great love and satisfaction as you guide and heal others. Your role is to be worked by being an example or model through your own experiences. We are happy that you'll be communicating with us more regularly.

Some messages will be pages and pages. It is as though they have finally gained your attention and don't want you to stop! You are, however, in charge of the reading and you can take intermissions. They will come back later and continue where they left off!

One thought or one element has permeated every one of the thousands of first messages our students have received: *love, support, and gratitude for the initial contact.*

It has been our experience that prior to receiving answers to detailed questions or specific encouragement regarding one's lifework, angels first establish a loving rapport with us. They have a single agenda: loving–supporting–helping. They are never further away than our next thought. They have no calendar or clock, never tire or grow weary, and always rejoice when we call on them. Their messages also have a single source, God, for the angels are His messengers, created to help and guide us while in this physical life.

We will work with you
whether you are
aware of us or not.
And how will you
know it is us?
When the possibilities
are limitless.

chapter 5

How You
Receive
Messages

◆━◈━◆

We are positive energy. We are light.

Your first angel messages or writings may not produce many words. You may think you have not received anything! We have seen students in classes look at their paper and appear bewildered as the scratching of everyone else's pen sounds like a roar.

Everyone connects with the angels, but not everyone accepts that they can hear them. Knowing how you receive your message will help.

Here are the three ways you receive angelic messages:

CLAIRVOYANCE
The ability to see things not visible to the naked eye. Second sight.
CLAIRAUDIENCE
The ability to hear sounds not heard by the human ear.
CLAIRSENTIENCE
The awareness of knowing beyond the five human senses. The sixth sense. Knowing that you know.

Clairvoyance is seeing what is not there. For instance, let's say the word being sent to you is "bell." You see in your mind a bell and know you are to write that word. The type of bell is significant, for example, jingle bell, Big Ben, or school bell. The bell you see relates to the message.

Clairaudience is hearing what is not there. Most often, you will hear the actual words spoken as given or dictated to you. This is a typical way to receive when you first begin hearing.

Clairaudience, however, also works with other sounds. You will not see a bell, but you hear the sound it makes. Again, the message dictates the type of bell. Do you hear a telephone ringing? Is it a bicycle bell you hear? A wedding bell? Whatever you hear, you will know to write the word "bell."

Clairsentience is "knowing that you know" and you don't have the foggiest idea *how* you know. This is a combined use of all the senses and is the greatest gift. If you are clairsentient, you may be expecting more at the start because you don't hear any sounds or cute little words being whispered in your ears. You just know what to write. Even if you are clairvoyant or clairaudient, your clairsentience will become stronger and you will soon use all the senses, including taste, touch, and smell.

If you experience a particular feeling while you are receiving, consider first that you may be receiving with clairsentience. If the feeling is positive, enjoy it! If the feeling is sad or painful, ask the angels to help you get rid of it or to explain it. Let's say you have a headache. The first thing to do is say, "Angels, if this is not *my* headache, please remove it from me now!" Clairsentient people are very empathic and tend to scoop up energy that is free-floating until they learn to control it better or to filter what belongs in the message and what doesn't. You may actually be feeling the headache of the person next to you, not your own.

Clairsentience is the most total gift and there are millions of you out there with it. We come to and through you all the time in this way.

Know what your primary gifts are. Practice separating multiple gifts. Trust your gifts at all times. When you go into a room and feel negativity, perhaps it isn't you, but the emotion of the group. Leave. There is no reason to stay in negativity. In life there are two sides, light and shadow. Choose light and people of light with whom to associate and spread light wherever you go.

If you think you are not receiving perhaps you are making the process of receiving angel messages unnecessarily difficult. Watch for:

Doubt:

Stop erasing as the angels speak. You receive the message just fine and then begin to think about it, question it, and talk yourself out of an accurate angel communication. What is sent in, leaves through doubt. Also, you edit the words to fit your opinions of life and your self-image. In one class, the angels gave a student her best qualities. She heard well and recorded an accurate list, but then editorialized and added her own opinion. When her angel said,

You are very patient . . . , she added . . . except when you are tired.

You are kind . . . to most people.

You are smart . . . when you want to be.

Angels do not give and then take away. They give with love and truth. They see you as you really are, not as you believe you are. They see you as a perfectly created person. You see yourself as imperfect. They see your great potential. You see yourself with limits. They see you as love and light while you may see yourself in despair and darkness. You are perfect today. You are on your way up. You are in a constant state of growth and improvement. As is the rest of the universe.

Poor Reception:

Angels work on your energy. If you don't hear them, *breathe.* More likely, they are not loud enough for you to hear. Ask them to speak up, to take turns, or slow down. It is a two-way communication and sometimes reception needs to be discussed and then fine-tuned. If you still can't hear them, ask to speak to another angel. You are in charge of the communication.

Keri was a frequent student at our classes. She came to class nearly every week but never heard really well. Finally, she came to us and asked if she was doing something wrong. We assured her she wasn't and we decided to talk to her angel for her to find out why she was not connecting. We could not hear her angel either! Only about every third word made sense. In frustration, we said, "Come on, angels, we need someone louder. Send an angel with a bigger voice!" A booming-voiced angel came in with a wonderful, clear, exciting, and comforting message.

What was wrong? Nothing. The angel with whom Keri had connected was a very tiny angel named Amelia. She was dainty and feminine and had a little voice to go with her diminutive body. When we found out what Amelia's work was, everyone understood why her voice was difficult to hear. Amelia's primary job in the universe is to whisper into the ears of babies how much God loves them.

Expectations:

— ✦ —

What you receive is what the angels want to tell you. It may be a simple or a complicated message. Trust and accept what is given. Angels also have frames of reference different from ours. Don't ask your angel about other people because angels will not engage in "psychic gossip." If you receive a message about someone else, know it is their angel that sent it.

Wrong Information:

— ✦ —

If you feel the angels give you wrong information, know that most beings on the other side are simple loving souls who know nothing about computers or politics. If you want to know more about specific knowledge, ask for a specific angel who has that wisdom. They will not be able to send advanced esoteric information if it is not their information too. If you don't speak French, they will not speak to you in French vibrations.

Engineers have angels who are interested in engineering and have helped them become an engineer. Same with doctors, chefs, teachers, and artists. You attach to each other because of similar interests. Mary frequently comes to comfort worried mothers because she relates so well to motherhood. Favored teachers, saints, or gurus will teach you because you already have a trusting relationship.

Angels give you the best they have at that moment. But time doesn't mean much to them and specific events are not as important to them as they are to you. They look at a bigger picture. Angels are great teachers.

Attitude:

Be positive! The best way to ensure a clear loving message is to decide for a positive experience. Expect goodness to come. Expect beings of light. Expect high angelic presences. Expect love. If you are a frightened, negative person who expects the worst to happen at any moment, you may initially find more comfort in prayer. When you begin, ask your angels, "Please teach me about love that replaces fear and to have a positive attitude to replace my negative expectation."

Whether you speak to them or not, their comfort is always with you, has always been with you, and always will be with you. It shall be forever so.

*Prayer takes
but a breath
of a second.*

You cannot defend your
belief in us.
You cannot defend the
undefendable.

chapter 6

How You Know It's an Angel Message

↢ ❦ ↣

The uncertainties and doubt you go through in order to figure out if you are getting a true message. It will only be a short time and then you will know if the message that anyone has written is an angel's message. In time you become experienced enough to discern the differences between you and us.

In the beginning you will have doubts and many questions as to who is actually writing the message. Here are some things to look for in determining whether it is your message or from the angels.

The first thing you will do is question who wrote it. You don't feel as though you have written the words. You say, "Do you think I did this? Does this sound like me?" In fact, you deny you wrote it at all! "This isn't my writing. I don't use these words," you will say. Do not expect this feeling to ever go away. Even now, as this book is being written, the feeling of not having ownership of it is strong to us.

Angel Writing Styles

English (or whatever you speak for communication) is not an angel's first language. Every language is difficult to communicate within because angels use vibration and thought, which is clearer, cleaner, and faster.

Angels also send several ideas at the same time and occasionally the message is confusing. It is wonderful how well you still understand when this happens. Just write down what they send as best you can and enjoy it!

One of their favorite things to do is to expand the concept of a word by adding a suffix such as "-ment" or "-ness" to words that don't usually require them. For example, words angels like to use are "wonderment" or "truthness." If the words they make up increase understanding, they are pleased, for this is truly good reception. One time an angel said to Barbara, "Dear One, today you are full of notness." And, she was being negative that day!

Combined Words

You will "see/hear" them do this often. Where more than one word fits, angels expand the concept by using both of them. Time is saved and language is "enhanced/refined."

Angels also expand thought by using three words at a time. "Yes, yes, yes" is how they may answer a question when being emphatic. Expect triple answers when it's them.

Angels Talk Together

Sometimes you will get a sense that several angels are talking at once. Ask them to slow down and take turns. You will know when there is more than one speaking, for it sounds as though they are having a party. They are!

Angels Feel Different

Angels are not you. They don't *feel* like you. They access different parts of your brain than you do. They may make your heart beat faster when they are with you. Sometimes you will feel a shiver or tension in your body that lets you know they are there. You will sense if they are male, female, or neutral energy. You may know their appearance and whether they are big, small, bulky, airy, child-like. You may get a sense that they are a certain nationality, intelligence, or have specific interests.

Angels are like friends or relatives, different from yourself.

Angels Cannot Give Unasked-for Advice

They can give guidance and direction, if you ask for it. God's gift of free will is sanctified by Him, never to be touched. If you *ask* for advice or help, it is then invited and it may be given as loving support. Unsolicited advice is rarely offered unless it is part of a larger teaching.

If you want to know which vitamin to buy, they can recommend one. If you want to know how to raise your children, they will tell you a child's strengths and suggest supportive activities and help. If you want to know if you should quit your job or get a divorce, they will tell you to follow your inner knowing and help you define and understand your reasons. The decision to quit your job then becomes a part of your decision to get on with your path and accomplish your life's mission. These are questions of choice and free will. Angels are support systems of the highest order, but they cannot tell you what to do or how to live.

Many times their messages will help you clarify your path. At one point a woman asked, "Why can't he tell me he loves me?"

Their answer was, "Because he doesn't." Immediately she knew her relationship had grown to its highest point and could go no further. She then chose to leave. But they did not, and would not, tell her to leave her marriage. If she had asked if she should leave, the angels would have said something like, "Choice, dear one. Choice."

Angels Say, "Patience, Dear One" . . . A Lot!

We want everything to happen NOW! Life is a process that makes sense in spite of how it sometimes appears.

When you feel you are receiving advice or direction of a more firm nature than angels use, then it is your higher self that is working. Again, always for your greater good, but your higher self is more demanding of you than an angel would ever be. The higher self knows all your life lessons and is intimately acquainted with your path. You usually know you are doing something against your higher self because you become miserable when off-track. Angels don't "give" misery, for angels are only love.

For fun, get out a box of colors, chalk, or markers and a big sheet of paper. Sit and be still for a while. Then, ask for our help and draw a picture of your highest self. A most interesting project in learning more about you. Draw a picture of us too. And what you see from the inside of your eyes. And what love looks like.

Please
quit worrying
about political conditions,
earthquakes, money,
jobs, relationships.
You have been taught that
no obstacle is too great
to overcome.
This is the truth:
There is no obstacle!

chapter 7

People Questions
and
Angel Answers

The most useful thing angels do is answer questions. They love to teach! Following are some of the most frequently asked questions in our classes.

Q. How many angels do I have?

There is a heavenly chorus that surrounds earth and helps mankind to evolve. This musical, playful, loving array of angels is but a tiny piece of the depth of help available at all times. Angels abound! Not in ones and twos, but in millions, billions, and quadrillions. Times twelve. Human beings are limiting. You say, "Do I have an angel?" It is as though you are not worthy of even one. We say it is not how many, but how deep. And the depth is unto infinity. An infinity of angels surrounds you as you do your work. We stand from here to God to help you. It is only in your mind do you feel alone and apart from us.

One special angel, or a billion angels, it is the same. We are loving support for you. Your work is our play. We carry energy, ideas, inspiration, love and joy from God, through you, to others.

Angels only individualize so you may be aware of our specific characters of helpingness. For instance, when you find a teaching angel or a warrior angel, we come into your presence depicting what we do best. We assume the look that suits your need. We add a name (as angels) so you may tell us apart. We do not need to be apart, but humans like to personalize, therefore we do that for your understanding. Later, as you get to know us and trust us, there will no longer be a need to separate us one from another. We will integrate into your intelligence as an "isness" when acceptance of us and what we do evolves into an inner knowing.

Masters, guides and teachers are very much individuals. Therefore, they come to you as separate energies because they are souls and no two souls are alike. Without ego, they are perfect helpers, for their only need is to help you when you require their particular essence or experience. Do not mix up angels, masters and your departed loved ones.

Quit asking "How?"

We are the How.

Q. Can everybody write to their angels?

It is not a matter of can you, but will you? The energy that surrounds the earth is opening to divine presence and we angels are doing our best to communicate with you, teach you, and help you through this time of spiritual searching. Many are being awakened as Barbara and Trudy were and as you are.

Q. Why should we write to the angels?

We always infuse you with love and this will concentrate our power. But when you write, we all focus. You and the facets of you, plus __us__. It is like the difference between air and wind. The power is added and you are the beneficiary. All is there for a greater good plus __power__. Know and believe this, for it is important. So important that we always come to you when you ask us to.

The act of writing to your angels means you do not have to wait passively for guidance. You can take the initiative and actively ask for help, for understanding, and for love. The answer you receive, when written, then becomes a permanent record that you can read and reread.

Q. Whom do we pray to, now that we know the angels?

God. Always God. Your highest belief. Your highest power. We pray to God. God is the source and

90

cannot ever be mistaken for less. Imagine a core in the universe. A center point upon which all else focuses and from which all else emanates. That is God. The All.

Q. Can human beings be angels?

People who have made their transitions may be angels as Barbara and Trudy refer to them as—with a small "a." Loving angelic helpers on the other side. But divine Angel beings, the messengers of God, do not incarnate on earth. Their work is to help and support mankind and to be intermediaries for God's love, help, and teachings.

Q. What is the difference between my spirit guide and my guardian angel?

They are a totally different species. As a human is different from an Angel, so a spirit guide is different. Spirit guides have lived on earth at some time and have taken responsibility to help you in your lifework. They are loving helpers. Guardian Angels have not been human, but are intermediary beings between God and man, specifically you.

Q. Do animals have angels?

All of God's creations have angels. Sometimes angels attach to pets specifically to work their love for you through your cat, dog, bird, horse, fish, etc. Love comes in every way imaginable.

Q. I think my grandmother is my Guardian Angel. I am aware of her presence.

Your grandmother is with you a lot because she loves you and has a strong connection with you. She is there to help you. However, in the strictest definition, she is not your guardian angel. She would be what is known as a spiritual guide.

Q. Has my Guardian Angel seen *everything* I've ever done?

Yes, but not to worry. Your Guardian Angel's main job is to love you unconditionally. No matter how ashamed you may be of some of your earth actions, your guardian only looks upon you as a seeker of truth. Seeking takes us down many paths. One thing is also true, that you cannot live in the light if you have not looked into the darkness. The nature of life is to know the edges of choice. As wisdom comes from choice, so does choice lead to wisdom. Just know that every soul on earth and those who have been here at one time or another have learned about wrong choices. You have not done anything worse than another. And nothing makes you less lovable in God's *eyes or in your Guardian Angel's opinion. They love you unconditionally and that means they love you no matter what.*

Q. What if I sit down to write and no one is there?

One of us is always there. Barbara and Trudy were worried about this too at the beginning, but it has never happened! If it should happen to you, take a nap. It probably means you are tired and you are not in a receiving mode. After you rest, take three deep breaths and begin again. We come in to you on breath, so be sure to breathe!

Q. What if they tell me something bad?

And what could that be? That you have judged yourself harshly? That you do not love yourself? We cannot even scold you, child. All we can do is help you find your truth. Decide to be loved by us, and you will not even be able to think we could tell you something bad. If you do get less than a loving message, it is not from us.

Q. What if I get a negative energy?

Pray and choose good energy only. It is very un-likely you would get a negative energy. If this should happen, invite this energy out. Tell it to go to the light! Stop writing, pray, and invite your highest angel presences to be with you now!

Q. How do I know if it's them or me?

Your own mind chatter is not as focused as our messages. Mostly know that our messages have questions behind them. And they are _your_ questions. When it is us, you aren't sure you wrote what you received. When it is mind chatter, there is never a question as to who thinks these words. If you doubt, then it is probably us.

Q. What is the difference between my higher self and my angels?

Your higher self is a composite of all that you are, have ever been, and ever will be. Your higher self is within. Angels are without. They are helpers. Your higher self is you. Your higher self is found in meditation more than in writing. Both are wisdom.

Q. Will my angel give me lottery numbers?

Probably not. The purpose of angelic presence is to give love, support, and teachings. Angels are not really very interested in lotteries. Our work has more to do with your soul.

Q. What my angel said would happen and what happened were not the same. How come? Did my angel lie to me?

We tell you the best we know at the time. We angels have a wider vision of the big picture, but we cannot interfere with free will. If events do not happen when you think they should or when we predicted them, know that the greater good of God was still being served. Always remember this very important thing: the universe is in a constant state of improvement. What once seemed to be for your greater good may not happen because of newer understanding or because of a different unfolding of events. Be flexible and know that each day is complete. Live in your nowness and you will find joy and spiritual purpose while walking your life's path, wherever it takes you.

Q. My angel never tells me anything interesting. I don't get very good messages.

Then ask for another teacher to come to you, child. We are not all tuned in to the questions you want answered. There are whole choirs of us who do nothing more than love you. We do not talk much when this is our work. Also, at the beginning, when you are learning to open your receptors, your messages may seem simple. Later, when you are more open and practiced, the messages will become more like "teachings." It is a learning process. The more you speak to us, the better and longer the messages get. Barbara's and Trudy's first messages were short and simple.

Q. My angel's answers are *very* short.

Then ask questions that require longer answers. If you ask questions that require short answers, like yes or no, that is what you will get. Some of you write such loooooooong questions it is more like journaling. Perhaps the most important part of the communication with us is to hear yourself ask the questions. This is all right and there is clarifying value in asking questions. But look upon our communication as a dialogue and you will see that you talk, we talk, you talk, we talk longer. Ask a question. Let the answer happen. Also, we notice some of you shut us off before we are done! Patience, dear ones.

Q. How come everyone else's answers are better than mine?

They aren't. It is just part of your need to receive affirmation that your messages are real that creates this question. Other angelwriters probably think yours are better than theirs. If you still think so, ask for a teaching angel to come through. They are the talkers!

Q. What does my angel look like?

There is an angel for every look and it will show his/her appearance to you when the time is right. You have many. Some are like little lights. Others are huge beings so beautiful you cannot imagine. You will be shown when it is time for you to know.

Q. My angel wrote to me in poetry. Can this be true?

Yes. We sometimes write in song lyrics too. We enjoy the different forms of expression that we can show. We give you what you need, and if you enjoy rhymes, it is likely we will come through in this manner. Expect anything from us.

Barbara has an angel who stutters. When he speaks to Barbara, her typing is terrible! Another angel always spells the greeting, "Hellow." He is identified that way. We are as diverse as you are.

Watch, also, for accents. Isn't it amazing that you will hear a brogue or a dialect when you receive us? At one class, a fourteen-year-old girl received her Grandfather, who was a salty old guy. His language was quite spicy, but to his granddaughter, it was a true message, for it was by his swearing she knew it was him.

Q. All my angels tell me to do is love. I hate that.

Yes, we are sure you do dislike that. Patience, child, there will come a day when you will understand. It is not far away.

Q. People say angels are "New Age." Are they?

And what, child, is this thing called New Age? The books of the Bible, when first written down, had to be hidden away for safety. New Age is a term given to unprecedented information. Angels are as old as can be. Love is not new. It is the same as always. God loving you, you loving each other. Love transcends every age. Angels are love.

Q. Please speak to me about death.

And what is this thing you call death? Death, child, is despair of the heart. Death is emptiness of the soul. Death is loneliness of the spirit. There is no death per se. There is only blackness from belonging to no light. When people come to you in their mourning and grieving and ask you, "What is my way? How do I understand?," then answer them that their way is always the correct one. Keep your work and way constantly pure and in the light. For in the light, there is

*no death. Only the everlasting, ever-growing aware-
ness of God.*

Q. I am skeptical about communicating with
anyone but God. Can you answer my
reservation and help me to better
understand?

*God is pleased you are careful not to give homage to
false messengers. We are, indeed, as close to you as
flesh is to your skin, and have been since before you
were born. We are like an umbilical cord connecting
the messages of the Father to you. These messages
are not of our own. They come directly from the Father. All the love, nourishment, and guidance is sent
through us to you because you are not able to understand or comprehend on the Father's frequency yet.
You must learn to be patient and discipline your
senses so that you will truly know within your heart
that what comes to you is truly from the Father and
from no one else. When you ask a child to listen to you
so he does not get hurt, and he refuses to listen, is it
your fault that he got hurt? It is the child's own free
will that hurts him. So too it is that you have your own
free will to hear the messages the Father sends to you
through us. Or to dismiss them. With time and discipline we will all be on the same frequency with the
Father.*

No one is going to
miss their mission.
Everyone does it in one
way or another.
All you need to do is say
"Yes" to it and
You will be doing it.

chapter 8

Angel Experiences of Real People

——✦——

Writing the angels can change your life. We have seen it happen over and over again. There would be no reason to communicate with them if there was not a practical reason to do so. Here are some stories of ways angels have worked for people to help them in their lives. Angels are beneficial and can literally get you through any circumstance.

Chris H.'s Story:

——✦——

In 1985, I had my first occurrence with cancer. I was thirty-two years old, considered myself healthy and active, and never thought it would happen to me. I was shocked and lonely and I was afraid to die. I couldn't even talk about it.

Today, nine years later, I am facing a recurrence of the same type of cancer, but my feelings are totally different because now I write to my angels!

At some point in the intervening years, I had a crisis of faith with God. When hurtful things happened, I couldn't seem to access comfort from Him. He seemed so far away. It was time for the angels to come to me.

Sometimes I felt vain to want God to listen to me. He is so busy! The angels seem more accessible. I'm much more aware of angels and I know I am being heard by them. I believe the angels *take* my prayer to God. It's a more believable and personal system. I used to ask for little things like parking places and they were there. Now I ask for help with my cancer, and they are still there. There is an army of them and I am protected by their vigilance. I feel as though they won't let anything harm me.

The angels have opened up my life tremendously and they come to me in many ways. I believe the angels come to me through the nurses. I see angels in my room, and angels come to me tangibly in cards, pins, statues, and pictures. Doctors, family, and friends have always been there for me, but this second time around I need more. The angels are the *more*.

I am much less afraid this time. I feel secure and protected. Healing is stronger and there is less pain. I have the courage to talk about my cancer and I even demand to take an active part in my recovery. I'm more away from my head and into my heart. I'm calmer and more settled in every area of my life.

The angels told me to use the word H A R K to remind myself they are there.

Dear Chrissie,

You know we love you and are proud of you.
H - Hear us.
A - Ask for us to come to you.
R - Release your worries and doubts.
K - Keep doing it.

This is how to work with us.

My life has always been a roller coaster, but I've liked the ride. Since my recurrence, everything has justified this belief and I can still say I like the ride. No matter what happens, I say to myself, "Okay, I'll learn from this too." The angels and I can do anything!

Dodd's Story:

Dateline: 8:14 P.M., Sunday, December 31

I was sitting quietly alone listening to my stereo and reading one of my favorite books, when a feeling of discontent washed through me. Why was I alone on New Year's Eve? Self-choice? Yes, but was it something I would have chosen if someone had offered me an alternative?

Was I unhappy? No. I was pleased with the simplicity and completeness of my accommodations. I had expected work—I was on call—and had therefore made no conflicting plans. Why, then, this wash of dissatisfaction? Did I want a lady on my arm to salve my ego? I didn't think so—I would have called someone if I had.

But a mate? A heart partner in that solid, complete, caring, satisfying, like-we-dreamed-about-when-we-were-young sense? Well, maybe, MAYBE!

Barbara Mark had told me there were four steps to getting your angels to help you: 1) Ask and be specific in your request. 2) Believe your request will be provided. 3) Accept the gift. 4) Give thanks.

Okay, so I can invent my mate. I liked this. What did I want? All of it.

She would be:

1. Bright, intelligent, and fun
2. Attractive to my eye
3. Living a healthy lifestyle
4. Experienced, sexy, and sensuous
5. Classy in a stylish sense but sedate and not flashy
6. A mother, with two children please, a boy and a girl (not noisy or unruly)
7. Artistic and creative
8. Concerned with and committed to personal growth
9. Spiritual—believing in a universal connection of mankind
10. Of the belief that people are more important than things
11. An athlete who will understand my training and support the effort
12. A morning person—4:00 A.M. is my wake-up time

I thought, "Ha! There you are, angels. Go for it!"

Dateline: 8:14 P.M., Monday, January 1

I was walking alone at the beach. I had known her before, but only as friends. It seemed she came from nowhere as she appeared at my side and said quietly and simply, "I'm glad to see you." We talked into the evening—of many things. She asked about New Year's resolutions. I told her what I had thought about a mate. She asked if she was part of the plan. I said no. We spent a languorous, luscious evening together. It was a wondrous moment in time. That was all.

Dateline: 9:47 A.M., Tuesday, January 2

A fire raged through my body. My skin felt inflamed. I was breathless, afraid, and joyous at the same time. I realized, "She is not *part of* the plan, she is the plan!"

Check this:

This woman is youthful, attractive, rows competitively and has won trophies. She is a CPA and has two delightful, smart, caring children—a boy, eleven, and a girl, fourteen. She is the height of decorum in public and sensual at home. She is interested in ideas and thoughts, believes in God, angels and spirituality, and is active in personal growth. She is caring, warm, intelligent, thoughtful, strong, joyful, and excitingly creative. Watercolor painting and poetry writing are two of her accomplishments.

Affirmations are her gift to mankind. Love is her gift to me.

Angels, I accept this gift and give thanks. She is in the room with me right now. I am still breathless.

Jackie's Story:

When I first saw angels, I thought I was hallucinating. The night I saw them, I had been out late and I was tired. While I was trying to sleep, they kept coming to me and comforting me. It was all night long and I was annoyed at the activity so I didn't let them into my consciousness very far. I was only twenty-one and I had no idea what was happening.

About 6:00 A.M., Mom opened my bedroom door and said, "Daddy has died."

I said, "I know."

Now, I believe the angels were hugging me and consoling me and lovingly preparing me for my father's passing.

I remember my room as being very light that night, while it was usually quite dark. I remember lots of movement and the sense there were so *many* of them. I also remember I couldn't get to sleep because of the activity in the room. That night changed my life forever.

For years afterward I asked others what had happened. I talked to some members of different religions, but no one ever had an answer to satisfy me. What finally made me aware was when I started writing the angels. I knew immediately it was the same group of beings that had been with me the night Daddy had died.

When Mom was dying, I saw the angels come and get her. Again, I didn't know it was the angels then, but now I do. It was the most beautiful, most gorgeous thing to see her lose the agony and the pain. She hadn't quit breathing yet, and I was telling her it was time to go. I saw her surrender herself to her angels. All of a sudden I saw acceptance in her face.

From time to time my angels have visited me without my understanding who they were. Writing to them made the final connection. I had been afraid of them because I didn't understand.

I have found I have always been what Barbara and Trudy call *clairsentient*. I have a way of just knowing things, but the things I *knew* scared me because I didn't understand. Now, when I put my questions on paper, the angels explain to me what is happening and I'm not afraid at all.

The best part of knowing and writing your angels is that they are so useful. What at one time I had thought was a hallucination, is now a part of my understanding of life. I'm not alone, I am not abandoned, and I am safe. I can't imagine life without my angels.

Lindy's Story:

I first experienced "writing to the angels" with Barbara sitting at her computer. Barbara had been telling me about the wonderful messages she was getting and had shared some of them with me. I believed, then, as I do now, that they were true angelic messages.

Before I began to write to the angels for myself, I would occasionally sit with Barbara as she typed out the messages. I would ask questions. The angels had been telling me to "enroll in something" and I thought art therapy was as good as anything. I'll never forget the day I asked, "What about art therapy?" I had been considering the course. The instant angelic reply was: "What about music therapy?" followed by a pause.

The pause was important because I had never considered music therapy and had no idea where to seek out a class. And then, on the same newspaper page as the art therapy class, there was an ad for a one-day workshop with the title "Changing Your Life Through Music and Imagination." I sent in my enrollment the next day.

If the story ended here, it would still show angelic guidance. But the story does not end here.

I learned, in that one-day workshop, that music is a powerful therapeutic technique and can be used with imagery to heal. I was so impressed with the workshop that I enrolled in a five-day session to learn to do the technique for others. During that workshop, I met several women who have become my best friends.

With the angels' encouragement, I went on to a seven-day intensive workshop, and am currently participating in a two-year internship that will culminate in my becoming a certified therapist. One of the requirements for certification is to have a master's degree in a psychology-related field, so I have also committed to returning to school for my master's degree.

Today, I often sit at the computer to get a message from the angels. I have received direction, support, counseling, suggestions for positive changes in my life, occasional gentle criticisms, and more love and comfort than I could imagine.

I had no idea, when I sat next to Barbara back in the spring of 1992, that the message I got would change my life. I was complacent in a job I'd had for nearly twenty years. I had no plans to return to graduate school. Now, thanks to "writing to the angels," I know what I want to be when I grow up. I feel a renewed sense of purpose. I am excited about returning to school and entering a new career. Yes, the music therapy workshop was about "changing your life," but I wouldn't have been there without angelic guidance. Thanks, angels.

Bob's Story:

I had been writing to the angels for several months, but not without significant skepticism. Prayer had been an integral part of my life since childhood and the idea of expecting "hard" information from any being but God was not palatable. Nonetheless, I continued to write because the messages I received were comforting and calming during a time of severe personal anguish.

Julie, my beautiful thirty-two-year-old daughter-in-law and mother of our only grandchild, was in remission after a year-long bout with cervical cancer. The medical reports looked favorable and our hearts were full of thanks for her recovery.

Early one morning I went to our home computer and asked the angels, "What would you like to teach me today?" At the time I was just about finished teaching a two-year course in "Care Giving" at my local church.

"Study the lesson plan on Grief and reteach it, Dear One." I wasn't interested in reteaching that chapter. Every angel message I received over the next several days spoke on the same subject. Three books on grief that I had bought but never read suddenly appeared on my desk. One morning, I tucked the smallest of the books on grief into my briefcase to read "in case the trip was boring." The train was five hours late that day and I was able to finish the book before I arrived at my job.

Several days later I was told that new cancer had been found in Julie's vital organs. New surgery and aggressive treatments were ordered. During her therapy, we shared a great deal of time together, in person and on the phone. We talked about our faith and our dreams for the future about our children. We talked about life missions and what we had accomplished. It was hard for Julie to believe that she could have had a life-assignment to *teach love* . . . much less that she had successfully completed her mission at such a young age. *But she had.*

My son called in early December during the season's worst snowstorm and told me that Julie had taken a big "left-hand turn." He asked me how soon I could be there. The angels had previously told me that I would be with Julie when she passed over. But with the storm closing in I thought that was impossible. The airports had closed and my only alternative was to drive!

Under normal circumstances, it was a twelve-hour trip. I felt if I was going to get through I had to go immediately despite the storm. After a quick meal I left determined to see Julie, to tell her I loved her, and to share our faith once more. And I wanted to be there to support my son and granddaughter.

The angels kept assuring me that I would be there in time. I passed hardly a car or truck as I drove through the night, stopping only twice for fuel. Days later I learned that ten minutes after I crossed the Hudson River, I-80 was closed for eighteen hours. Had I not left when I did, I would not have seen Julie alive. I was never drowsy, never felt alone, never without a song or psalm, and never without my angels in the car throughout the night.

I spent the last hours of Julie's life with her. I saw her squint her eyes at what must have been a bright light and reach out a hand to touch an angel who came to greet her. The last words I spoke to her were, "The Lord is my light and my salvation, whom shall I fear? The Lord is the strength of my life, of whom shall I be afraid?"

Julie passed over on December 15, 1992, from extreme pain into exquisite peace, her mission completed.

The preparation I received from the angels for Julie's passing significantly altered the course of my life. After returning home, I have helped others work through their grief processes. Promises the angels made to me concerning the trip were all true, and I learned to understand the angels as part of God's divine plan.

Tom and Chris V.'s Story:

We had been trying to buy a house for several years, but our special needs and individual desire always stood in the way of our finding the perfect place. Finally, we decided to just turn the "house problem" over to the angels.

First, we decided to ASK as we had been taught in class. So, we made a list of exactly what we wanted in a house.

1. Three bedrooms—one for a bedroom and one each for a personal area
2. Backyard
3. Fireplace
4. Unpainted woodwork and built-ins
5. Tile that was old but in good shape
6. Lots of windows
7. Patio
8. All the appliances necessary to run a house
9. View
10. The lowest possible fair price

We found the house the first weekend we seriously looked. When we drove by the house the first time, we immediately knew it was the kind of place we wanted. As we walked around the house peeking in the windows, Chris tried the back door. It was open! It was our first introduction to our new home and we were able to go in by ourselves. Our first thought was, WOW! It was magical. There was a special energy associated with the house that we couldn't resist and we found ourselves driving by again and again over the next few days. It was like the house had a spiritual energy that enticed us to go back and look at it one more time, but we were worried about the feasibility of the whole idea because the house was more than we felt we could afford. The angels encouraged us to make an offer by introducing us to the perfect real estate agent. She was our "angel" on earth.

As first-time buyers we had no idea how complicated the house-buying process could be. At one point everything fell apart. The seller wouldn't communicate with our agent for six weeks to accept or reject our offer. We had given notice at our apartment and were being held to our word when we had said we would be out by December 13. It was the end of November and still no word from the seller. We were even considering upping our own offer in order to move the owner into answering us. We wanted it that badly! But every time we met with a glitch or a problem, we gave it to our angels and the problem melted away.

Eventually we purchased our perfect home for $20,000 less than the seller had paid for it several years ago. He even repaired items we didn't ask him to. When we settled for one set of terms from a loan institution, our agent called and said she had found a better deal. Our house payment has ended up being *less* than the rent we had been paying.

The only compromise we made was that there was no view, but we decided to forgo the view when we saw the terrific backyard with fantastic flowers, plantings, trees—even a magnificent pepper tree! Now, when we look out the window into the backyard, we realize we really did get a view, just not a long-range one.

If you want to buy or sell a house, get your angels on your side. Be receptive to the signs that they are working for you. Watch for the people being sent to you. Keep your mind open so you won't miss the guidance you are receiving. Many times our angels worked through others and set things up behind the scenes. A window of opportunity would open and a previous problem would disappear. The timing was critical many times and we never could have arranged it so perfectly.

We love our home. People coming to visit us talk about how right it is for us and how good it feels to be a guest. The combination of the energy of us and the energy of the house is perfect. We are glad we asked and believed. Letting it happen was the scariest part. But now we are sure saying Thank You!

Carol's Story:

For two months I had hives. Then came the debilitating muscle and joint pains, the sore throats and the spiking fevers. Finally, I ended up in the hospital for two weeks. Twenty doctors examined me and I had what is called the "million-dollar workup." I apparently had an infection, but they couldn't find the source. Antibiotics didn't stop the symptoms. Steroids did. The hospital released me with no concrete diagnosis. My medication was the steroid prednisone, enough to damage my body if I were to stay on it for any length of time.

Trudy suggested we ask the "angels" to help us understand what was happening. The answer we received was a little surprising. They said that I had a "parasitic infection from wine bottled in South America" and that it would be "difficult to diagnose in this country." When asked how long I would be ill, they said, "It will take its course and will be done with by the new month."

My husband's reaction was a sarcastic "Uh-huh." My friend Patty said, "I can't take this angel thing. It's just too bizarre." Our friendship of ten years ceased.

It has been eleven months since the first of the hives appeared. Last week doctor number 27 called. He is from Mexico and was recommended to me by a *new* friend. "Guess what," he said. "I found you have a *rare parasite."* Since my job as a flight attendant placed me on planes that had traveled to South America, he felt that the parasite I had picked up probably came from one of my flights. "Ahh!" I shouted. "The angels were right!"

During this time of illness and frustration, I learned to rely on meditation for relaxation, strength, and peace. Meditation has become a vehicle for me to become close to God, my guides, and my angels.

I ran into Patty the other day. We haven't spoken to each other since October. It is now mid-June. Patty asked how I was feeling. I answered, "Better. I just found out I have a rare parasite that can easily be treated."

Her jaw dropped. Then she simply said, "I can't

believe it. How could they have missed it all these months?"

I loved the opportunity to answer, "Obviously they didn't ask their angels!" Thank you, Angels, for that scrumptious moment of joy.

There is equally as much love in this world as there is pain. Do you not believe this? Love is shown daily in the most abundant amounts to the sick, old, homeless, dying. And by whom is this love given? This love is given in copious amounts by the sick, old, homeless, and dying. The meanest hovel on earth has love in abundance. Love begets love. Your angel's mission is love. Your mission is to continue it.

These are your only
tasks in life:
1. Be Available.
2. Love.
There is no other
plan needed.

chapter 9

Our Angel Experience

<hr />

We are probably much like you are. In our own lives, it has been difficult for us to learn to accept all the abundance the angels have to give. We limit ourselves just as much as you do, even though we have been taught over and over that the angels have an unlimited supply of goodness to bring to each of us. The story of how this book came to be written serves as the best example to us as to how the angels continually give more than we would think to ask for.

After we had taught for a while, the angels told us we would write a book to share the *Angelspeake* method with those who could not attend our classes. We were told they would provide a perfect environment at a time when we would be together to receive the book. We were also clearly told the book would be written quickly and that we were not to be concerned about content or format.

Most surprising of all, our angels assured us that a publisher would accept the manuscript in a *day* and that the *right people* would be sent to us to make all this happen. We were dubious! We thought we had to "do something"!

In March 1994 a woman from *Good Morning America* called Trudy to say that they were planning a week-long series on Spirituality in America and wanted to include a segment about angels. When the producer learned that Barbara was teaching angel classes in Wyoming at the time, the show sent a camera crew, a producer, an on-camera correspondent, and Trudy to Big Horn, Wyoming, to tape a jointly taught class. The show, which aired on May 1, gave millions of viewers a real grassroots angel experience from the actual class we taught in a wonderful hunting lodge.

It took five hours to complete the taping and there were scores of interruptions. But we learned that when the angels work, they work! Every student received an angel message, as usual, and the experience was not marred by the confusion of taping.

The owner of the lodge invited us to continue our stay as long as necessary in order to write the book our angels had promised. It was a perfect spot, right at the foot of the Big Horn Mountains on the historic Bozeman Trail. There were deer running through the fields in front of the lodge, and pheasants came  clear up onto the porch to greet all the angels who had gathered. We had everything we could possibly eat and all the time we needed to work on this book without distractions of any kind.

The first day nothing. The angels said, *Rest and take walks.*

The second day, again nothing. The angels said, *Don't worry, when the time is correct, we will begin. Just rest.*

The third day, nothing happened. We began to worry. We had come to this wonderful setting, had experienced the thrill of teaching together for television, had scores of angel assurances that we were to complete this book . . . and nothing was happening! The angels simply said, *Continue to relax and be patient, children, for you are being made ready to receive our information and guidance.*

The fourth day, like impatient children, we sat at the computer and asked, "Angels, what is going on? When are we supposed to begin?"

Their booming reply was, *Are you ready? Start with Chapter 1. Then Chapter 2, then 3, etc. Don't look back.* And the book began. One sister received information for a while and then the other would sit at the computer and receive. This book was truly a joint project from beginning to end. Barbara, Trudy, and our angels.

Before we left Wyoming we said our thank-you to the angels (and our hosts) and then asked for the correct agent and publisher to be put into our lives to get *Angelspeake* published!

In the months that followed, there were times when it seemed like no progress was taking place and we were no closer to seeing the book published than when we left Wyoming. But all the time our angels were there with us, calming our fears and encouraging us to be patient. We had to keep reminding ourselves this book was not our book, but God's book that the angels had helped us to write. We kept receiving daily messages telling us, *All is going well. There are circumstances occurring, children, that you know nothing about. Patience.*

But it was hard.

Agents did come to us as we had been promised. We never had to seek them out and they were perfect for our needs. They had little knowledge or belief in angels when we met, but they were experienced in book publishing and were enormously helpful in every step of the process.

In another reading, the angels said the actual publisher would come through a contact made by Bob, Trudy's husband. True to the angels' word, it did. While working on a church project, the minister suggested Bob call an editor he knew at Simon & Schuster. The following Thursday, the book was sent to the editor in the morning, was accepted that afternoon, and we confirmed the offer that evening. Truly, as the angels had said, the book was accepted in a day!

Our final message to you is to ask you to allow the angels to be part of your life. When you do, miracles truly happen. You will be amazed how much joy and comfort they will bring, how much support and guidance you will receive, and how your life will be filled with love and peace.

We were told, *We will bring you more than you will ever think to ask for.*

They always have.

Here is their ending message to you.

Angel Touches

Think of a time when an idea came to you
that was so vivid and pure and was so true for you
rolls of shivers started in one part of your body and
then inundated every cell of your being.
You may call that
Angeltouches
or
Loverushes.
That was Us.
Think of a time when you awakened at night
with a thought so clear
you knew it answered your every question.
That was Us.
Think of a time when you were so still
you could hear
music and knew it was the "music of the spheres."
That was Us.
Think of a time when you loved so totally
you could not express it

for there were no words invented
to translate the feeling.
That was Us.
Think of a time when the earth,
and God,
and You
were so aligned that you knew it was your truth
in all its glory.
That was Us.
Think of peace so deep
you could not reach the bottom of it.
That was Us.
Think of a time you were so connected with love
and light
you said you were filled with God
or the Holy Spirit.
You were.
But it was also Us.
We are not hard to find.
We are there in the stillness.
We are there in the waiting.
We are there in the knowing.
Just BE.
We are there.

About the Authors

Barbara Mark and Trudy Griswold are sisters who have helped people throughout the United States to gain new understanding of themselves by teaching classes in Angel communication techniques. Barbara and Trudy were featured on *Good Morning America,* where their workshop on how to contact Angels was part of a series called "Spirituality in America." Barbara lives in San Diego, California, and Trudy lives in Westport, Connecticut.